Blindfolded

Blindfolded

HOW A YOUNG MAN FOUND
THE COURAGE TO SEE

Courtland J. Manning

ISBN-13: 9780692818961
ISBN-10: 0692818960

To those who always believed and didn't let me go down the wrong path.

To my mother, with love. Thank you!

Contents

Introduction

I am releasing this book to celebrate my graduation from the University of Colorado Boulder in December 2016. As with any great milestone, it is important to reflect. Truth be told, statistics would tell you that I should still be in the same place I grew up—or broke, or in jail…or even dead, as some believed. I have prevailed despite the odds. It has become a passion of mine to share my story with today's youth so they may learn from the lessons I had to learn the hard way. My story is not a pretty one, but it's an important one to tell. Hindsight is crystal clear, and I see now that only a few things matter above all. One of these, as you will come to discover, is listening to the voice within that tells us we are destined for greater things despite the odds that may be stacked against us. In pivotal moments up to this point, I have listened to that voice and followed it.

The following are real accounts of my life experiences. Some names have been changed out of respect for the privacy of the individuals. Everything I recount in this book has been specifically chosen for the purpose of telling my story in a concise and forward manner. Many experiences and people have not been mentioned, but that does not mean they did not have a significant impact on my life.

I look forward to sharing this story with you—a story I consider a testament to the power of will, determination, and listening to the voice within.

CHAPTER 1

Life Choices

I was born on January 9, 1995,
at 1:22 p.m. My mother was
only twelve years old.

B ack in those days, even more than today, having a
child at such a young age was unheard of. Those
who didn't know her jumped to conclusions about
who she was—her morals, her background, her upbringing.

And to those who *did* know her, it was an absolute surprise. The truth is, my mother was a good girl. She never slept over at anyone's house. She never gave anyone more affection than a friendly nod. She held strong to her morals, knew right from wrong. She didn't trust just anyone. But after one sleepover—just one time—she got pregnant.

So contrary was this to her true self that she actually never even considered she could be pregnant. Such a thing typically isn't on the radar at that age. It was actually her mother (my grandma) who first suspected. To find out for sure, she told my mother that she was giving her a pregnancy test to evaluate her iron levels. The test was positive. She was just in seventh grade, her whole life ahead of her…and here they were, staring at that positive sign that would change everything. Disappointment, disappointment. Shame.

My grandma Brenda and my great-grandma Mary took my mother to the doctor to confirm the results. My mother described the doctor as an older woman— white hair, very tall, very skinny, wearing a long white coat. Immediately upon seeing my mother and discerning her young age, the doctor asked my grandma Brenda and great-grandma Mary to leave the room so she could speak to my mother privately. As the door shut, the doctor turned to face her.

"Honey," she said, taking her spot on the navy-blue rolling chair in the corner, "I want you to know that this is your decision and yours alone. No one else can influence or make this decision for you."

I can see my mother now, fidgeting on the scratchy white sheet on the doctor's table, knobby knees on those barely teenage legs dangling, not yet even able to reach the floor. Staring wide-eyed at the doctor, hanging on every word she said. Looking for guidance and finding support…but understanding that the decision was truly in her hands alone.

The doctor went on. "But you are only twelve, and your body is not yet developed. Honey, you are still only a child. If you choose to go through with this pregnancy, it's going to be very hard on both you and your baby. You can give up your child for adoption right when he or she is born, or you can choose to have an abortion now. The choice is yours."

My mom took a moment, hands clasped on her knees, eyes staring at the white, pixelated floor. The doctor rubbed her back, reassuring her, and my mom heard these words, spoken softly over and over again: "Whatever you decide to do is fine."

Meanwhile, in the waiting room, my grandma Brenda was pacing back and forth, praying fervently. "Oh, please, God, help her make the right choice." With every pace, she passed my great-grandmother, who was sitting down, praying for the same thing. This girl, my mother, was the center of their world and had barely even begun to know herself. A decision like this was more than a twelve-year-old could make—it was an adult decision in the hands of a child. A choice of this magnitude had implications far beyond what she could immediately see. What would the complications be? How would this hurt her body? Frankly, could she survive a pregnancy and still be the same? These are questions they could only give to God and pray that she made the right decision.

The prayers came together, and my mom reached a decision she would never once turn back on. She looked up into the doctor's eyes, shaking but certain, and said, "Doc, I want to have him."

"Are you sure?" the doctor whispered without breaking her gaze.

"Yes, I'm positive," my mother replied.

"Well, okay." Her doctor smiled with resolution as she helped her off the table. As they walked into the waiting room, my mother announced her decision. A smile broke across my grandma's face as she ran toward her with relief, hugging and rubbing her back. She would later tell me that she felt a release, because despite the objectivity she was praying with in asking for the right decision, she deeply hoped her daughter would choose to keep the child. Simultaneously, my great-grandmother raised her hands to the heavens and exalted, "Praise the Lord! Thank you, Jesus—you always come through!"

Thinking back on this pivotal moment, knowing who I am now and how where I come from has shaped me, I find a security in knowing that my mother made that decision and never looked back. She never believed she'd made a mistake—she trusted in herself and knew it was the right thing to do. And she was supported in that. If she hadn't made such a wise and mature decision at just twelve years of age, I wouldn't be here today.

This got me thinking about the power of life and how we all came to arrive on this earth. What a gift life is, even if it's not always apparent to us. Regardless of what has transpired since that decision was made, I will always love, admire, and appreciate my mother's heart and desire to have me even though she had every reason not to. She sacrificed her childhood and her independence. She had no idea how to be a mother. She had two easier choices: adoption or abortion. And yet she chose *me*. She believed that God had blessed her with a son who was going to be special. Knowing that has had a huge impact on my life and how I view myself.

I believe we are all here for a reason, and we all have a purpose to serve. We come from different places and have different parents, different upbringings. But the fact that we are all here *means* something, and we can't deny that. In more ways than one, we faced adversity to get this point. Something so much bigger played into what brought us here—something bigger than we can comprehend. We are living and breathing on this earth today because we are special. All of us. We are on this earth to leave it better than it was before we arrived. We do this just by being who we are, but the impact we can have is in direct proportion to how much energy we exert into fulfilling our purpose. We are equipped with the talent and gifts to bless the earth with our purpose.

The key is finding that purpose, which we must do. As humans who have been blessed with the gift of life, it is our responsibility to fulfill it.

So that was the beginning, and in retrospect, it brings my understanding into hyper focus. There have been lots of ups and downs since, but regardless—my life has been a very special, magical experience. And depending on the lens you view your own life through, I think you'll find the same. As I share my story, I want you to understand that I went through many challenges and witnessed many atrocities that no person, let alone a child, should go through or see. But in the retrospect, my vision is clear. It's made me who I am, and it's made my story. And in sharing mine, I know you'll see your own story in a new way.

You see, my mom operated on the belief that God and the universe wouldn't give her a situation she couldn't handle. "Too much" would not be put on her plate. And more than just that, no situation would be imposed on her that wasn't supposed to occur. I was supposed to be born, and she believed that. It's what willed her to unselfishly make the decision to have me.

Through my time so far, I have come to see that the great tragedy is the large number of individuals who wake up every morning and go to sleep every night, just existing. There is a wide gap between *existing* and *living*. When we exist, we are merely going to school and going to work. Going through the motions. Doing what we have to do. Repeating the routine. But when we find our purpose—the reason we were placed on this earth—then we are living. The great challenge is to find that purpose…and for most people, that doesn't happen. From watching the adults around me, I know that when you're living paycheck to paycheck, you lack the time and luxury to consider your purpose or, if you come to know it, to work to achieve it. I had to find my purpose in all that mess and confusion, and I have come to see that my purpose has been defined by how I fought in the face of adversity and kept fighting through every obstacle. And I know I can encourage you to do the same. If I got through what I endured, as you will come to read about in the following chapters, then believe me when I say that you can, too. But I dare you to live through whatever comes. Don't just exist. *Live*. And that includes taking off that blindfold.

Because the fact that you are here is no mistake. So don't just fall into the routine of existence. Don't fall asleep every night only to wake up to the same day tomorrow. Take ownership. Wake up to live.

It's been just about twenty-two years since my mom found out she was pregnant and would be having a child. Today, our relationship continues, but I'd say it's a work in progress. Over the years, we have been through a lot together. I blamed her for a lot of the obstacles I faced as a child, and she has openly admitted to not always making the decision she knew would be right for me but rather the decision she wanted to make for herself. I haven't always felt that my mom loved me, because I couldn't understand why she'd do some of the things she did. However, I do realize that my mom was young and honestly had no clue how to raise a child. She was trying to figure it out for herself, so she surely didn't know how to teach a child life lessons or even how to live a good life. I have since forgiven my mom, because in spite of the obstacles, I feel that I'm a better person today for having endured them. Sometimes I feel like thanking her for everything, regardless whether the choices were good or bad, because if anything had been different, I would not be who I am today. One thing I used to say to myself then and continue to say to myself now is, "Tough times never last, but tough people do." My mom and I have gone through some tough times together, but because of them, we both stand stronger today.

CHAPTER 2
Troubled Waters

struggled a lot as a young boy. There was a dissonance between what I felt to be true in my heart and my surroundings. I knew that I was destined for greatness, but there was no role model for greatness around me. I knew I would one day be powerful, but I saw people around me attaining their power through drugs and violence. I knew I had something to give the world, but that was hard to implement when I couldn't even give my mom what she needed. When I was ten, I wasn't responsible for giving my mom anything, but I was able to realize that she didn't have what she needed to make ends meet for us. She just didn't have enough money. I made a decision then to do what I could to provide for us—and, naturally, I decided to do what I saw others around me doing.

We struggled financially as I was growing up, and looking back, I know my mom was doing the best she could. She was such a young mother that as she raised me, she was essentially raising herself as well. We had to learn together. I remember coming home from school and going to my room to watch a game when the electricity went out. On those hot summer nights, we'd wander around in the dark and muggy heat, just miserable. The food in the fridge would spoil, and we couldn't afford to buy more. I'd often have to walk to my cousin Ta'Shara's house to eat. For the most part, I had to learn to live *without*. My mom did, too. I distinctly remember coming home from school one night when I was in the third grade and seeing her on the couch, her head in her hands, crying. She didn't know how to provide for us, and I didn't either.

During this time in my life, my father wasn't around. He was incarcerated and therefore entirely unavailable to help us. I never felt that he was someone I could turn to for guidance, because he was never around and didn't seem to know right from wrong himself.

I remember feeling so angry all the time—I felt greatness in my heart, but life was devoid of opportunities to bring this greatness into manifestation. My environment made me small, and I didn't fit in the confines it trapped me in. I was bigger. I was uncomfortable. I was angry at my circumstances. I was mad at myself for feeling this sense of purpose in my heart that was not affirmed by anything in my life. Just as cold air meets hot air to create thunder, contradiction in one's life creates trouble.

Disillusioned, I resolved that this greatness, formerly thought to be inevitable, was simply not possible for me. This stripped me of all hope and put me in a position where I was malleable to any outside influence. I was with my mom often, and she would spend most of her time with her adult friends. She and her boyfriend had been friends with this group since high school and had stayed in the same circles, stuck in the same bad habits.

I automatically felt "cool" when I spent time around them. I figured that as a kid hanging out around adults, I'd learn more about power and influence—after all, they had more than I did because I was still so young. I think any kid likes hanging out with adults and learning from them. I watched how they acted and talked, and I emulated this in front of my friends. But beyond just mannerisms, several of them also had their hands dirty with drugs, so I watched the lifestyle of a drug dealer play out. Because I was looking up to them, I thought this was cool. I thought *they* were cool. And I wanted to be cool. These drug dealers, gangsters, and pimps were all very well respected in the community—they conjured a sense of power just because of what they were doing. They had the most money, which came from selling drugs and pimping out their prostitutes. I mistook my desire for greatness as a lust for power, deciding that I could attain power in the same way the adults did. It occurred to me that maybe this is where that feeling was coming from. Maybe this was where my dissatisfaction stemmed from. Maybe this could cure this deep-seated desire that had never been satisfied. Remember, this was the only role model for any type of greatness I had ever seen.

So I stole drugs from my mother's adult friends. I remember they were passed out from partying all night, and I knew they were careless about where they kept their drugs. I found one of their jackets and reached into the pocket, finding the Ziploc bag. I knew I could sell this to my friends and peers, both at school and in the after-school program. I remember telling my friends ahead of time that I was going to start doing this, because I wanted them to help me sell the drugs to make money.

I packed the bag tightly into my lunch box beneath my sandwich and placed the lunch box in my backpack. When I got to school, I remember taking my books and notepad out and placing my bag in my locker. I didn't touch it again for the entire day. I was terrified—I knew what I had in my bag could get me into trouble. I didn't really know *how much* trouble, though. I was just doing it because it granted me a sense of feigned power and the hope of being able to provide for my family. If I could save the money I was making, I reasoned, maybe I could help my mom pay the bills. Maybe I could help my mom put food on the table. Maybe then she wouldn't worry as much.

We could save up enough to move away from here and start a better life.

But then I was caught selling drugs. I was at the after-school program, and my mom had figured there was something off about how I was acting. She must have noticed my being overprotective of my bag and was curious to know if I had something in there I wasn't supposed to have. She let me go to school that day but sent Ta'Shara to pick me up from the after-school program, telling her to check my bag. When she came to get me and asked to see my bag, I told her no. She asked again, and I declined again. By this time, I was sure she was also curious to find out what I had to hide (now that it was clear I *had* something to hide), and so she just snatched the bag away from me. I vividly remember hoping she wouldn't take a peek into my lunch box, but once she'd unzipped and looked inside, she didn't seem to find anything suspicious. For a brief moment, I was relieved. But then, just before zipping up my bag and giving it back to me, a voice in her head must have said, "Check the lunch box!" because she suddenly reached back in and grabbed it. Opening it, she was immediately caught by surprise and at a loss for words. She looked at me and said, "You are going to be in big trouble." She took my bag with her to show my mom.

My mom did not find my desire to provide for her at all charming. Rather, she was disappointed and hurt. I remember her telling me that she wanted better for me, that she'd imagined better for her son when she made the decision to have him all those years ago. I felt touched by what she was saying, because I too wanted better for myself. But the truth was, I wasn't surrounded by better. The only "better" I could see was dealing drugs and making money through that means. It wasn't taboo in my community, and everyone seemed to be okay with the adults doing it. If it was okay for them, why wasn't it okay for me? I didn't understand.

I had originally decided to put it behind me, because I didn't want to see my mom disappointed. But then, Mom got into worse financial trouble. I once again felt helpless. By this time, I was in the fifth grade, and I had become a big brother, so it wasn't just me and my mom anymore. I had a baby sister, too, and I wanted to provide for her. I knew it was my mom's job to provide for us, but we were in this together—you have to be when you are struggling to get by. She couldn't sugarcoat the truth or pretend our circumstances were different than they were. I wanted to alleviate her worry, take the burden off her shoulders. I decided I would do it just one more time—just to make enough money to put some food on the table, to help with the bills. Same as last time. I believed it was worth it. At that time, I didn't care about any of the potential consequences. My life felt like it was over and not worth living, regardless what I did. We did what we could to get through each day, and that's as far as I could see—to the next day. To the next meal, whether it was there or not. To the next hour, if the electricity would stay on. To the next drug deal, if this one went well. I saw what I had to do to satisfy the next "next," and I went for it.

I set up a sale for after school and went to meet my friend. We quickly made the exchange. I was certain I was in the clear—until I saw a police officer out of the corner of my eye. I recognized him—he had volunteered at my after-school program. He knew me. He was younger himself, and I presumed he was new to the job. He raised his hand to wave hello, but I could tell from the suspicious look in his eye that he had seen the entire exchange.

"Hey, boy, what do you think you're doing?" his asked, his voice booming.

I didn't think. I just ran. I mean, for Pete's sake, I had just gotten caught! What were the chances I'd get caught twice in a row?

I heard his feet heavy and quick on the ground behind me as he tried to catch up.

"Boy, you better stop, or eventually I'll catch you! And when I do, you'll be in trouble!" he yelled.

It occurred to me that I should probably stop. I couldn't run all day, and the farther we got from the location of the exchange, the more trouble I imagined I'd be in. Don't anger a police officer who already has reason to arrest you. And it probably isn't a jog in the park to run after a quick boy like me in his full polyester uniform, gun, badge, and all.

So I stopped and turned around to face him. He stopped, too, relieved, and we faced each other for a moment, catching our breath.

"What are you doing?" he asked.

"Nothing," I sheepishly replied.

"I saw you," he warned.

"I wasn't doin' nothin'," I defiantly declared. He patted me down and searched me, ultimately finding the remainder of the drugs. I was expecting the hand-cuffs to come out at this moment, but what he did next surprised me. And truthfully, it changed the course of my life. He sat me down, looked at me intently, and said, "Son, do you have any idea how much trouble this drug dealing will get you in?"

"I know," I lied. But then I took a deep breath so I could tell him the truth. "My family needs the money." I really hadn't been aware of how much trouble I could have gotten into at the time—it could very well have become a downward spiral leading only to a life in pris-on. But that officer cared about the community and the people in it. I often think about what life would be like for me today if he hadn't seen better in me or if I had been caught by another officer who wasn't as understanding. There's no reason I shouldn't have been thrown in juvenile detention. From that day forward, I was more careful about avoiding trouble, figuring you only get one big break, and this had been mine.

He told me he understood why the stress on my family was affecting me but went on to say, "You could go to jail for life and then never be able to provide for your family in any real way. I believe in you. I've seen you at the after-school program. I know who you are, and I know that you are more than this. And the truth is, this one drug deal may be able to provide for you today, but what about tomorrow? How many times will you sell? How will you know when to stop? And every time you go out there to make an exchange, even if you think it's under the table, you run the risk of getting caught. And the consequences are dire, son. You could go to jail. Stay there for life."

I got the odd feeling that he was doing me a favor—not just out of the goodness of his heart but because he truly saw something in me that no one else seemed to see. Maybe he could see the greatness just beginning to take form. He ordered me to throw away the drugs and promise to never sell again. In return, he'd let me go.

"But if you ever—and I mean *ever*—sell again, I will arrest you," he warned.

Because he saw something more in me, I once again believed there were other ways to be successful. There are more honorable and fulfilling ways to make money and be influential. Just because I saw drug dealing around me didn't mean that was the only road to power. He had power as a police officer, and that had nothing to do with drugs or pimps. The trouble with being surrounded with only one type of person is just that: you can only desire to be that one type of person. You don't see any other paths cut out for you. But the police officer reassured me that it wasn't my path. And once we can stop going down the path we've been on, a new one can form beneath our feet. I actually never saw him again, but I know that if he saw me today, I would thank him for that pivotal moment. I think he would feel a sense of relief, knowing that his intuition about me was right. I hope he would be proud of me.

CHAPTER 3
Summer in Kansas

My experience with drug dealing was not my first experience getting in trouble. My tendency to misbehave started many years before, but my actions had been much more innocent than drug dealing and my brushes with federal law. I was really good at misbehaving, and I got in trouble all the time. My mom would get a call from the school every day explaining all the troublesome things I had done. I wasn't interested in school, so I wasn't doing the work. I refused to obey what the teachers said or to pay attention in class. My behavior became such a problem that I realized how it started to affect everyone around me. No one was more affected by it than my mom. Every time she got yet another call from the school, she would sit me down when I came home and give me yet another lecture. And those lectures didn't work. Whether she was stern and doing all the talking or just trying to have a meaningful conversation with me, it didn't get through to me. I would always hear my mom and other adults in my life say what it meant to be "good" and "moral," but then they'd always do the opposite. I saw the hypocrisy, and their words meant nothing to me. I consider myself to be observant, and I always watched what people around me were doing and tried to mimic them, whether it was good or bad. I heard what it meant to behave but saw what it was like to misbehave—and I decided to misbehave.

I was constantly grounded and in trouble, which meant I'd have to go without TV, my game system, or anything I liked to do. That deprivation didn't work either, but again, this was because I was following what my mom was doing, not necessarily what she was saying. As a kid, you view your parents or guardians as the most important people in your life. From the beginning, parents are in the most central position to influence what their child begins to think, believe, and do. I was looking to follow someone who was leading by example, and it was clear that following her and the other adults around wasn't leading me to make good choices or take smart actions. I was lost.

When I'd get home from school, I'd have to sit down and do my homework instead of spending time with my friends. Or I'd have to go to a reading program and read. It affected my football life, too—I couldn't go to football practice when I was in trouble, which meant I couldn't play in the games. Or if I could go to practice, my mom would pull the coach aside and tell him I'd been acting up. As punishment, my practice would consist of running by myself. Eventually, everyone got exhausted with it because no punishment seemed to work. I simply didn't care. I wanted to do things my way, even if that meant losing what I enjoyed and what was important to me.

My family decided that I probably needed to get away from the negative influences around me and spend some time in the fresh air. I was eight years old, and my family felt that the only thing left to do was to send me away to Kansas to live on my uncle Virgil's farm for the summer. Little did I know that this trip would become a consistent, annual trip. This first summer in Kansas, I was not yet selling drugs but was starting to get into the habit of getting into trouble. Later summers in Kansas would prove to be more beneficial, because by then I was getting into more and more trouble, so the time away became more important. I see the summers I spent in Kansas as the summers that kept me from getting into the most serious trouble. It kept me off the streets and kept me busy. My uncle Virgil gave me the structure and guidance I needed to take back home with me to try to stay out of trouble. In fact, the lessons I learned from Uncle Virgil still play a role in how I live my life today.

Uncle Virgil had spent many years in the military and had been planning to retire soon. His dream was to retire to the farm and be a farmer. He was just getting settled on his new farm when all my trouble was arising, and he was happy to have me and a few of my other cousins for extra hands on the field.

So on my last day of school before summer break, I went home and immediately packed up everything so

I'd be ready to go when Grandpa and Uncle Joe picked me up the next day to take me to the farm. They loved to drive, and whenever a family trip required driving for an extended period of time, you could count on Grandpa and Uncle Joe to get the job done. I absolutely did not want to go.

I wanted to spend the summer hanging out with my friends, but it was more than that—I actually *liked* getting in trouble. It was my way of getting attention, because I didn't feel like I was getting any at home. But when I got in trouble, my mom would pay attention to me because she would get upset. Getting in trouble didn't bother me, but I watched how it bothered the people around me, and this gave me some secret satisfaction. Honestly, I was angry at them, just as I was angry at my circumstances, and believed I was hurting them more than I was hurting myself, which actually was not the case. I was hurting myself more than I was hurting them. I was hurting myself more than anyone else.

Kansas was like going to summer camp, but instead of for just a few quick weeks, it was for the entire summer. Uncle Virgil's military background quickly snapped into gear. His philosophy was all about the value of hard work and discipline. He was a very serious man—definitely someone you couldn't play with. His stern nature demanded respect, and I in turn respected him. When I got in trouble, I could tell I was in for it before the words would come out of his mouth just because his eyes would get so big.

We'd wake up at five o'clock every morning and first work on our personal training, going for our morning run and then doing sets of push-ups, and sit-ups. Then we'd have a quick breakfast, and immediately afterward we'd be off to a day of work in the fields. We did everything you'd imagine in the field: cutting the grass, picking up poop, stacking barrels of hay, cleaning the truck...

One thing that really stands out for me about this first summer and Uncle Virgil is that he bought each of us a calf in order to learn responsibility. That was a really good idea, because you have to be responsible to raise a calf. It was much like raising a baby—we'd have to get bottles and mix the formula. The calf formula came in a bag the size of a bag of dog food, and the formula was actually similar to what you would use for a baby. In fact, the way we made the bottle was the exact same as you'd do it for a baby. It was like learning fatherhood and how to be responsible for a fragile life that depended on us. We'd scoop the formula up in a measuring cup, toss it into the bottle, and mix it with warm water. We'd then shake the bottle to make sure it was all mixed together. We'd have to wake up early to feed our calves and then come back to feed them multiple times during the day. We always made sure they were tended to and had what they needed. In addition, we did house chores to learn responsibility around the house. And then, outside the house, we were expected to go to church and Bible study. We were all on a very strict routine.

At the time, I considered this to be the worst summer of my life. But looking back now, I see that this summer (and all those to follow) was very beneficial for me. I came back home a changed person, more and more responsible after every summer. I wouldn't even realize it, but I was continuously changing for the better. I didn't get in trouble with the guys on the farm. Uncle Virgil made sure of that. He wanted us boys to grow up to be part of society, contributing to it rather than being menaces or detriments to it. He drove this point home by teaching us responsibility. I ended up spending every summer until high school started on the farm in Kansas with Uncle Virgil. And truthfully, I believe that if I hadn't done so— had I spent the summers running around with my friends—I could've gotten into much deeper trouble than losing TV privileges or getting a smack on the wrist.

I still think about the impact and value of those summers in Kansas. Now, all of my cousins who spent those summers with me are successful too—all of us in our own individual ways. But the point remains. It's exactly what Uncle Virgil wanted. Meanwhile, my other cousins who stayed at home did as I suspected I would have done—they got themselves into deeper trouble. Whenever I'd even think about misbehaving, I'd see Uncle Virgil's face or hear his voice warning me not to.

I can now have conversations with Uncle Virgil with more perspective and maturity, and his intentions on how he wanted to help us are even clearer to me now. I always tell him that the experience had perfect timing for me. Before then, I had been ready to keep getting into trouble, and this had been a critical juncture in my life that required action. My family noticed it and made it happen. And Uncle Virgil took it from there.

Now that I've had time to sit back and reflect, I realize that I carry the same vision that my family did for me. I didn't want to be the kid that was constantly getting in trouble. I wanted more for my life. I did not yet have a specific vision for my life, but that inner conflict needed to be resolved. And now that it has, I have clear vision. And most importantly, I learned the value of hard work in getting what you want. I've applied that every day since, and I owe my new successes to it.

CHAPTER 4
A Pivot in Direction

The summer after my freshman year of high school, things significantly turned around for me. Although I had long since given up my drug dealing and troublesome habits, I was still struggling with my inner voice that told me I was going to be great, as I had no idea how to bring that to fruition.

My two aunties had been in my life since the beginning and were very supportive figures in my upbringing.

They called me after school let out, informing me that I had no choice but to attend a week-long business camp that summer. I was adamantly against it. I didn't want to live in a dorm (it was on a college campus) with a roommate (I was used to sleeping on my own, thank you very much) and work from seven in the morning to seven at night every day. Frankly, it sounded like hell to me. But they meant it when they said I had no choice, and even though we bantered about it awhile longer, I ultimately lost the fight and found myself on that college campus. And boy, I'm glad I did. (I sometimes wish I could go back and tell my younger self to not waste the energy on putting up that fight. We all know there's nothing worse than admitting you were wrong.)

I look back on attending this camp as another pivotal, life-changing moment for me. My aunties had signed me up for it because they wanted me to have a new experience, something unlike any I'd had prior to that. And they wanted me to get out of my comfort zone. I knew it would push me, make me uncomfortable, and that's another reason I didn't want to go. I didn't know what to expect. I didn't want to experience discomfort or try anything new.

It was new because it was my first experience of devoting time to sessions on understanding success. Real success, building success, success beyond the "hood." There were sessions on branding, personal finance, and all aspects of entrepreneurship. I remember being amazed by the wealth of knowledge at my immediate disposal with the resources of this camp. Here were professors who gave their time and energy to students, investing in them. I was riveted from the first day onward. I entirely embraced the experience, thrilled to realize I was actually understanding the concepts—something I believed I could not do, as I had been told I had learning disorders and had had to take remedial classes in school. Remedial classes are designed for students who are thought to consistently underperform; consequently, the attitude is much more "do what it takes to get by" rather than encouraging greatness. This experience was different—they actually *wanted* us to succeed, and I was intrigued. I learned quickly because I was so fascinated with what I was learning. It became clear to me that I was grasping real business concepts that I could use for the rest of my life. I finally had the basis to form ideas on how to be great.

This greatness paralleled the greatness of my instructors. It was an entirely new type of greatness than any type I'd seen before. Yes, the instructors had just as much money and power as the drug dealers and gang leaders back home, but it was in an entirely different way. They led entirely different lives. They were making an impact with their money and power. What a way to live, I thought to myself.

See, my original conception of greatness had two end routes: either I'd end up in jail for an indefinite period of time, or I'd die. It's no secret that drug overdoses and street fights can be fatal. That split second of feeling great and powerful as you throw the punch is inconsequential when it's met with a gunshot or a stabbing. People act violently when they feel out of control and desperately want to take hold of the steering wheel of their life. I had found a new way to take control of my destiny.

The fulfillment I felt was unmatched. I knew that I had continued to listen to myself—and yes, I was destined for greatness. Yes, I could and would be great. I already was. And here was a real way to make it happen. Here was a way that would allow me to enjoy every second of my life, to feel powerful by empowering others, to make an impact, and to make enough money to support myself and my family. It was not until this new life panned before my eyes that I realized it: *I had been blindfolded.* It is impossible to realize how blind we've been until the blindfold comes off. My intuition reflected a life of greatness in high definition. How different this was from the way I had blindly stumbled through life before, following what was in front of me like a lost dog, praying the path in front of me would lead somewhere but yet always turning up empty handed. I had been guided by the Dead End and Caution signs stuck into my face by a life and a society that believed I was destined for nothing. But I knew better. I kept my hope alive.

I walked away from that week very excited because I knew I was onto something. I told myself, in that moment, that if I played my cards right from then on, I would be able to achieve everything I always knew I could. The rest of my life could be different. The blindfold was gone, and I now knew how I could be great. And now that I had seen it, I knew I would never blind myself again.

I had a knack for business, and this is something I never would otherwise have known because I had before never exposed to it. I don't think my aunties necessarily knew I'd have an aptitude for it and end up doing it for the rest of my life. I think they just wanted me to have a new experience, an experience that would get me out of my comfort zone.

You see, I view the comfort zone as the place where we're at a standstill. It's uncomfortable to move out of it because we aren't used to moving, and we're moving into uncharted territory. It's uncomfortable to embrace the unfamiliar because we're not sure how it will turn out. I urge you—make the moves. You'll end up surprising yourself. And even if it's not something you'd like to do again, you gain something from the experience.

Every time I've stepped out of my comfort zone, I have been stretched. Sometimes I've been stretched so far and so thinly that I didn't think I could make it through. But in hindsight, remembering all those times, I realize I *did* make it through. And beyond that, it made me grow enough to achieve my next challenge or next experience with more ease. We just have to keep going, keep stretching, keep growing. It enables us to engage in new ways. The most successful people tell me they constantly aim to step out of their comfort zones. If we don't grow, we can't succeed. And if we remain within our comfort zones, we don't learn, which in turn makes us obsolete. We are then living with our ego. "I don't need to be uncomfortable. I don't need to take this step. I'm happy right here." But we are bigger than that, and we were meant for more.

Aim to live a life that you can look back on, connecting the dots of these experiences and understanding how they forged the path to your ultimate success. You can't achieve your greatness if you aren't equipped with the experience to know how.

CHAPTER 5
The Power of Believing

n school, I wasn't considered even average. I was considered deficient. Deficient of talent, intellect, gifts—even the ability to cooperate or to be a good student. My teachers would always call my mom, informing her that the quality of my work was lacking and that I just wasn't getting it as easily as the other students were. And because I didn't excel, I concluded that school just wasn't for me. None of us *like* what we struggle with or what we don't do well. It didn't help that I was thrown into remedial classes without a second thought. No one took the time to help me; they just assumed that because I had been struggling, I always would struggle. I suppose I understand that. But you can't get someone out of their old habits and into a new routine without shaking things up a little bit.

Remedial classes move slowly and condense content. Talk about boring. I personally believe that if schools want their students to be engaged, the material should be exciting. But in the remedial classes, it wasn't about engaging or helping students to excel. It was simply about hoping they'd pass and giving them the barest bones of the information to make sure that would happen. As long as I was moving along and could maybe one day get a high school diploma...well, that was enough for the kids in the remedial classes.

In reflecting on how I became so discouraged and so out of touch with my studies, I now know that my homelife situation differed dramatically from that of my peers. I saw firsthand what adults had to deal with in the real world—*real* problems, not math problems. *Real* issues, not the kind you read about it in the assigned fiction books in English class. I had to worry about making it to the next day without the power going out again. And don't get me started on paying attention to a monotone voice reciting some lesson on decimals and reciprocals when I was hungry. When you're hungry like I was, all you can think about is eating. Math isn't really a priority in the face of hunger.

It's even worse to listen to a lesson in history when you're tired. And boy, it seemed I was always tired. I didn't sleep well at night because my mom and her boyfriend always had people over. I could hear them in the other room. Sometimes they would throw parties, and the noise would keep me alert until the early hours of the morning. I could also never fully relax, as on a number of different occasions, my mom would burst into my room and cry for hours after a fight with her boyfriend, urgently saying we needed to leave right then. I'd jump out of bed and throw everything I could into a bag that I kept near my bed. If Mom said we needed to go, we really needed to go.

On top of being hungry and extremely tired, I worried. I worried incessantly. Nothing in my life was stable, and I just didn't think school was important enough. No one thought I was talented or intelligent, so what was the point? And what was the point of trying today when, if we really had to move far away, I could possibly be at a new school tomorrow?

When I moved back to Colorado from North Carolina, I had to start at a new school. Awesome, right? Just what I wanted. Another school to evaluate my performance and state the obvious: I was underperforming. I wasn't smart. Got it. Maybe I should have just gone right in and told them to sign me up for the remedial classes and skip all the drama. As expected, my first semester didn't go well. By "didn't go well," I mean that my report card had a grand total of seven Fs on it. Seven. I remember my mom looking at it in disbelief, her face crumbling as she realized how badly I had failed. She didn't understand how it was possible to completely flunk every single class. In case you're wondering, here's how it's possible: you go to school and do nothing. You don't pay attention. You don't do the assignments. You just sit there, trying to ignore your grumbling stomach and your heavy eyelids and all the worries spinning through your head.

I made the conscious decision to not do anything, which really helped with the whole "sitting there" thing. I mean, at least I had an intention here. But in retrospect, I realized this "no can do" attitude was only hurting myself. I believed that if they didn't consider me smart enough, then I wasn't going to waste my time showing them that I was. What was the point? These were teachers who'd taught many students, all of whom performed better than I could. After one glance, they decided I wasn't smart or talented enough. And I was starting to believe that they were right.

That report card caused a real hassle in my family, and everyone seemed to have their own two cents to give me. I'd get some clichéd speech about the power of motivation, how I should really figure out a way to be more motivated and apply it to something that mattered. It still wasn't clicking for me, because it seemed to me that no one truly cared how I did in school or where an exceptional performance in school could get me. This was apparent by the superficiality of their speeches. Yes, you can sit someone down and try to motivate them with words. But what I really needed was for someone to take the time to sit down with me and help me master the concepts I wasn't understanding. I figured I was just in school because the law said I had to be, so I'd do what I needed to do to get by. I didn't get why everyone cared so much about the seven Fs, and it was beginning to occur to me that they cared about my academic performance more than I initially believed.

Somewhere along the way, I became tired of underperforming. I realized that if I didn't at least perform well in my remedial classes, I may be moved to simpler remedial classes. I remember a conversation with my uncle, who knew I had heard it all before. So, in his simple, encouraging way, he urged, "You don't need me to tell you to do what you need to do. You already know. I encourage you. You're better than this."

That conversation came just when the wheels had started turning in my head, and I realized once and for all that I had to get it together. So I went to every one of my teachers for an individual conversation, and I let them know I had taken some time to reflect on my performance. I was ready and willing to do better. To my surprise, the teachers reacted well, granting me not only forgiveness but the chance to make up work. I was sent home for Christmas break with study materials and worksheets. I planned on completing five sheets per day so I could be finished by the time I got back to school. It was the first time I had held myself accountable.

Those worksheets and tests were not perfect—there were scatters of Ds and Cs—but plainly and simply, I wasn't failing anymore. I was improving. My hard work had tangible results that made me and my family proud. And that was enough to motivate me even more. I realized I had to continue improving in order to prove to my teachers I was deserving of the opportunity they had allotted me. What this really came down to was my attitude. When people say attitude is everything, it's because attitude is *truly* everything. Suddenly, I wanted my teachers to believe in me. I wanted to be in the regular classes with my friends. I wanted to learn. I wanted to surprise everyone. The only problem was that I didn't know how to be a better student. I had never been taught. I had never developed those habits.

But one teacher seemed to have the same attitude toward the year that I did. He was a new teacher, and he was out to prove himself. I could see it in his eyes. I saw my new self and my new intentions in him. He had this raw energy—he wanted the other teachers and the administration to be impressed with him, and he'd do whatever it took to achieve that. It was a business class, which I was proficient in. I had a real knack and interest for business, especially after that summer camp. I knew that's what I ultimately wanted to do with my life. He came to recognize this in me, so he would take the time to talk with me about it. We'd talk about the stock market—bear market, bull market—and he'd talk to me as if I were an expert, not just a student. He talked to me like an equal.

One day, after I shared with him some of my background, he disclosed to me that he too was from the hood. But he wanted to know more about me, because he saw more in me than where I was from. It was more important to him to know where I was going. He expressed a genuine interest in me—something I had never seen from a teacher before. He cared about my capacity for success in a way I hadn't seen with my other teachers. It wasn't feigned. He had a similar family situation, a similar background, and he recognized this. "We're the same, C. J.," he'd say to me. I found this empowering. "I don't really know you, but I want you to know you're special."

He was the first person to ever say this to me. No one else had taken the time to get to know me, and just from a few conversations, he saw something in me that no one else had seen before. What power we give someone when we tell them that they're special! If he could see it in me, maybe I could try to see it in myself. Maybe I could really believe I was.

He knew I struggled with believing that about myself, so he constantly reminded me that he needed me to believe. He became my support system throughout that year. It wasn't until I experienced this type of support that I understood how detrimental it had been for me to *not* be believed in. My teachers hadn't believed I could be a good student. If they didn't, I sure as hell couldn't.

Part of me couldn't help but think, is this man crazy? Does he know me at all? Is he seeing what everyone else is seeing? He had to prove to me why I should believe I was special, and he did so by committing the time to working with me, talking with me, and seeing me as a multifaceted human being with real struggles and real hopes. So I believed.

Belief is powerful because it's grounded in what's inside us. The teachers at my school knew my story and knew my struggle. They knew where I came from and how the story ends for most students who come from the hood. They saw my learning disabilities and labeled me for that. "Garbage." "Trash." "Not good for anything." But Mr. Baird taught me that all I needed to realize was that I was valuable despite these labels. Just because they didn't see my capabilities didn't mean I didn't possess them. Mr. Baird saw it differently—he saw the labels *and* the story as the ingredients for my ultimate success. Yeah, maybe I had learning difficulties. But I had been through more than anyone else had, and because I was still standing on my two feet, I had something to show for myself. This isn't something that could be seen on the outside, and Mr. Baird always reminded me that what was valuable about me was on the inside. That can't be touched by labels.

Because he saw me as a future college student that would get a degree, I started thinking accordingly. I saw myself as a college student. I saw myself as successful.

And thoughts translated into action. As I began to live into what I wanted to be, it translated into how people saw me. I wasn't trash anymore. I was proving my value—because I knew my value.

So don't let anyone label you. No one can label you if they didn't make you, because they don't know what's on the inside. Even if they look at you and think they have it all figured out, that is nothing more than stereotypes. Let me make an example here. If you were to go to the meat aisle in a grocery store and pick out a package of organic bacon, you'd see the label "Organic Bacon" and believe that it is organic bacon. We know this because we assume that the person who labeled that bacon had to make the bacon to know that it's organic and would label it accordingly. I share this example so you can understand that no one can make accurate snap judgments of you just by looking at your cover or even by making assumptions. The only person who knows for sure that the bacon is organic is the person who raised the pigs and sliced the bacon. Seeing is different from knowing, but we just see and assume we know.

So no one can decide just by seeing me, or seeing you, whether or not we are successes. There's a flip side, too. Now that I've had some experiences with success, people look at me as someone who's a success already. That comes with its own labels, too. They imagine I'm from a rich family, have had opportunities my whole life, and never had to work for anything. But that's not my story at all. So no matter what, don't let anyone label you if they didn't make you.

CHAPTER 6
Open Arms

After my summer in Kansas, when I was still just eight years old, I began going to the Boys & Girls Club that had just opened in my neighborhood in Denver. A certain man came to visit us there often. He had an air of importance about him. Every time he'd walk through the double-door entrance, everyone would whisper and watch. He was like a celebrity. One day, I asked my friend who he was, and he told me he used to play for the Broncos. Not only did his football career impress me but also something I noticed in the way he carried himself. He always looked so dapper, so well put together. His clothes were classy and clean, he spoke well, and his intellect was sharp. He really seemed to take care of himself. He stuck out like a sore thumb in my neck of the woods, and I instantly knew I wanted to be like him.

When you see people you want to be like, you want to spend time around them so you can memorize their mannerisms and bask in their personalities. I'd watch this man play games with the other kids and help them with their homework. I noticed that he came every Wednesday, and this soon became my favorite day of the week. That was the day I could play games with him, and I started working on my homework with him as well. Over time, we ended up becoming closer and closer.

One day, he asked me if I'd like to help him out with something. Of course I did! I'd do anything for this man, and I was honored that he asked me. He told me they were shooting a commercial for the Boys & Girls Club and asked if I'd like to be in it. I said I'd love to.

As a thank you, he invited me to go to a Broncos game with him. I had never been to one before but had always wanted to go. I remember being very excited. I knew that since he was taking me, I had to look just as well put together as he did. I found my best outfit, and I made sure to wash and iron my clothes. That morning, I showered, brushed my teeth, and put on lotion. The game was everything I'd hoped it would be—and more— and I felt extra special that he'd asked me to be his guest.

We stayed connected through that string of Wednesdays, and I remember he would always ask me about school and my life. I'd often lie to him and say things were okay when they really weren't. I wasn't lying to pretend to be something I wasn't; I just didn't want to tell him how things actually were for me at home. Three years later, he asked me to be in another commercial with him. Again I was very excited—this meant I'd probably get to attend another game with him! Naturally, he asked me after the commercial to come to the game, and it was just as fun as the first time. I picked my finest outfit and looked my best. I always tried to be my best with Mr. Thompson, because he always tried (and succeeded) to be *his* best. I observed how respected and adored he was, and I remember thinking that I wanted to be respected and adored in the same way.

Over time, our friendship grew, and eventually he asked me over to his house for holidays and weekends with his family. Spending time at his house with his family was the polar opposite of my life at home. I never had to worry at his house the way I had to worry at mine. The electricity wouldn't go out, there would always be plenty of food, and they made sure to get me everything I needed—clothes, school supplies, you name it. Eventually, I started to open up to them about my family life. They were upset that I hadn't told them previously, but they understood. To my surprise, they asked me to come live with them permanently. I imagined what that would be like, living a life without worry, where everything is taken care of. I imagined entire weeks of enjoying the same ease as the weekends and holidays I'd spent with them.

See, whenever Mr. Thompson would drive me home on Sundays, entering my own house would be like a slap in the face. Reality would sink back in. I was back to restless nights and worrying about how the next day would be. This began to seriously interrupt not only my school life but also my beliefs about my potential. Things were so hard that I suppose it was natural to be pessimistic. I just didn't see a way out.

I didn't think moving in with Mr. Thompson was the answer, either, because I knew my mom needed me. And I knew I'd miss her. I'd miss my friends, too. Mr. Thompson also told me several times that living under his roof would come with some strict rules and that they'd be hard on me. I had come this far without anyone being hard on me, and I liked that freedom. I didn't want to give that up. I declined their offer.

Eventually, things got worse for me. My home life was entirely draining. We were constantly moving. My performance in school started to decline again. I'd spend five of the seven days in the week with my family, and they never saw the same light in me that the Thompson family or Mr. Baird saw. I began wondering if I should give up again.

How fortunate I was to have had another place to go, because I know others often aren't as lucky. I knew I needed to move in with the Thompsons, at least for a little while. I decided to give it a test run for one week…and that week was the best in my life to that point. I was pleasantly surprised at how much easier it was to live and function without the incessant worry. Without all the worry, my head was clear. I felt I could now make a decision about how to move forward. It was clear that I needed to move in—for good.

Mr. Thompson drove me home that Sunday, but only so I could grab the rest of my bags. On my way out the door, my mom stopped me.

"C. J., where are you going?" she asked. I told her I was leaving to live with Mr. Thompson, and she was not pleased. I told her I needed a different life, that I needed to surround myself with people and circumstances that were consistent with the life I wanted to live. Ultimately, she let me go. I think she understood. Either that or she could tell I had a new sense of urgency about me. What else would prompt a sixteen-year-old to leave home so young? I knew I had a small window of time to take the steps necessary to get into college and get a scholarship. It was hard to leave my family, because I didn't want to seem ungrateful. The fact is, I was very grateful for everything they'd given me, but I knew a better life waited for me outside of that house. I knew a better life was mine to have. I deserved it.

The Thompsons invested a lot in me—I call them my parents for a reason. They didn't need to take me in. Mr. Thompson didn't have to volunteer his time at the Boys & Girls Club, let alone go to such lengths to help me change my life. But they did. They showed me another side to life when times were dire, when I felt lost and discouraged. They gave me the spark to light my fire, to forge ahead, and to achieve my greatness.

No amount of gratitude is enough. The only thing I can do is continue to grow myself, live the best life I can, and be the best version of myself possible—for them. I can pay it forward and one day invest in a child I believe in. I will light the same spark in that child that they lit in me. They did all they could to allow my light to shine, and that's the thing about light—it grows and spreads rapidly, affecting everyone in its path, making for a better tomorrow.

To this day, the Thompsons are still some of the most important people in my life. I know firsthand that many kids out there grow up in families that don't have the means to support them or give them a good education, and that's exactly what the Thompsons did for me, even though they didn't have to. It felt natural that they were my parents, and sometimes I'd even forget they weren't my biological parents. It became hard to distinguish between them and my real parents. They had a genuineness that was sparked by their belief in me.

I have been very fortunate to have many mentors in my life who took me under their wing and helped me achieve success. Where I came from, I didn't have the means, but I have been able to find many people who are able to see themselves in me and therefore want to invest in me. Keep in mind that my mom never went to college. My dad was never around, and he didn't even finish high school. They weren't able to give me any knowledge or insight to help me on my educational journey. But when you allow yourself to be mentored and guided by others, you have access to new resources and ways of thinking that you may have not considered before.

I see mentorship as a way to give children and individuals growth opportunities. I have been connected to people who have helped me grow. Without their support and investment, I wouldn't be who I am today. The only way I can pay them back is to pay it forward.

You don't have to think of it as mentoring; rather, think of it as allowing others who have achieved success to influence your life. It's allowing them to teach from their perspectives and experiences. Because they are older and have been through more, chances are they've been through what you are going through now or what you are yet to go through. You can avoid mistakes they may have made because they are there to share their expertise. You stand on the shoulders of giants, so you can realize your own greatness. We all help one another.

When Mr. Thompson first walked into the room that day at the Boys & Girls Club, I didn't know his story or who he was. He just had an air about him that proclaimed greatness, and everyone recognized it. Because I wanted the same for myself, I clung to him and let him influence my life's path. We hear all the time that in order to be successful, you have to be around successful people. You have to mirror them— think like them, act like them, speak like them, stand like them. Prior to joining Mr. Thompson's circle, I had never seen what it takes to be successful. So connect yourself with the successful people in your circle, and allow them to help you build your life.

CHAPTER 7
Time for a Change

Flash forward to my senior year of high school, when self-belief proved to be the best attitude I could develop. Not only was I in regular classes instead of remedial, I was in some honor classes as well and was already taking college classes for college credit. I had gone from that report card of all Fs to the opportunity to have a serious conversation about college possibilities. Mr. Baird was still in my life, mentoring me and guiding me onward. I still didn't think I could go to college, but he sat me down and said to me, "C. J., look what you've been able to do." He was right.

So when it came time for my senior meeting with my high school counselor, I had clarity about what I wanted to do. When he asked me where I wanted to go to college, I confidently replied, "The University of Colorado Boulder to study business."

He looked at me hesitantly.

"Do you know what that takes?" he asked, his tone dripping with condescension.

"Yes—a 3.8 GPA and a 28 on the ACT," I recited from my research.

"Which you, my friend, do not have," he cautioned.

Remember what I said about a dose of self-belief? I had enough of it from my teacher's encouragement to say these next words: "I believe I can get there, because I've turned things around."

"Well, your chances of acceptance are slim, so if I were you, I wouldn't focus my attention on getting in. Rather, I'd advise looking at community colleges. Then you can try to transfer after a year or two," he said.

"No, I believe I can get in," I replied firmly.

He sighed, looked at me intently, and then took his glasses off and leaned on the desk closer to me.

"All right, then how do you expect to pay for this expensive school?" he asked, coming at me again.

"With a scholarship," I replied smugly.

"Do you know which you'll be applying for?" he asked.

"Yes—the Daniels Fund." The Daniels Fund provides full-ride scholarships to any school in the United States.

"Only five percent of applicants receive the Daniels Fund," he warned. "So I wouldn't focus my attention on getting that. It's great you've identified it, but the truth is…you aren't going to get it."

I did exactly what he urged me not to do and focused all my attention on it. Mr. Baird truly believed that I would get into CU Boulder and that I would get the Daniels Fund scholarship to help me attend. I focused my attention on it because when I even just thought about the possibility, I felt the same feeling of determination swelling inside me that I'd had my whole life—a belief that greatness was my destiny and that I would find a way to be great. I didn't want to believe otherwise. Had thought I couldn't get it, I would have been devoid of self-belief. So despite my counselor's admittedly valid points, I continued to believe. And when I faltered, my teacher continued to help me believe. "CU will be lucky to have a student like you," he'd say. "And the Daniels Fund will be lucky to give a scholarship to you. Your doing what you've done makes you different," he'd tell me in encouragement. "You're not like the rest of the students. You were put here on this earth to be great. I need you to believe."

Originally, I hadn't been like the rest of the students because I was lesser—less talented, less smart, less capable. That's what the teachers had believed. Beliefs aren't always right, and we can't waste our lives letting other people's opinions define us. This is why we have to cultivate self-belief and stay close to those who believe in us, even when we don't believe in ourselves. To Mr. Baird, I wasn't like the rest of the students because I was special. And that made all the difference. "If you're not going to believe for yourself, believe for me," he'd say.

One day, I came home from school to find a letter on the counter from CU Boulder. I knew it would be either my acceptance letter...or my rejection letter. My fate was in that envelope. My heart jumped to my throat. This was it. I tore the envelope open and fumbled with the papers, my shaking hands unfolding it.

Dear Courtland James,

Congratulations! You have been accepted into the Leeds School of Business at the University of Colorado Boulder…

I promptly dropped the paper, fell to the floor, put my head in my hands, and cried. The impossible had happened. The impossible wasn't impossible anymore. It was more than a belief now—it was a reality. And in my relief and ecstasy, I felt gratitude for the teacher who had believed. I had no idea how he'd known, but he had. And he showed me how to know, too.

I made a photocopy of the acceptance letter and slipped it under the door to my high school counselor's office the next day. I wanted to show him that my self-belief was more powerful than the beliefs he had about me. I could do it. I had proved him wrong.

The next month, my great-grandma Mary called and said, "Baby, we have a letter from the Daniels Fund here for you." Everything stopped...or slowed down... or...I'm still not sure, because my panic in that moment silenced and numbed everything in my reality.

"Would you mind opening it and reading it to me?" I asked her. Over the phone, I heard the fumbling with the papers, and then she read the date, and then the address, and then...

Dear Courtland,
Congratulations. You are a recipient of the Daniels Fund scholarship...

I didn't hear the rest because the phone had fallen from my open hand. I once again shed tears of joy. Only 5 percent of applicants receive that scholarship...and they had chosen me. Me! The one who had been in remedial classes, who was considered less than the other students.

I had achieved greatness for the first time in my life, and that initial taste was worth all the years of wanting. I knew that because I had achieved this, there was *nothing* I couldn't achieve. And further, I knew I achieved this because someone had believed I could.

Take my word for it—we are all destined for unique types of greatness in our own life paths. If everyone were the same and achieved the same greatness, then nothing in life would be interesting. Don't get me wrong, I still have all the same learning disabilities—ADHD, dyslexia—but because I know I can achieve, and because I know I'm smart, those seem inconsequential.

After one great achievement, others come more naturally. I started to walk, talk, and act like a great achiever—I began to *become* a great achiever. Sometimes I still struggle, but I'm committed to being great where I'm destined to be. So I urge you—invite difficulty. Embrace the struggle. In the midst of it all, you will prove to yourself that you deserve that self-belief. It is all an inner battle. Mr. Baird taught me I was great, and so I say the same to you. Believe.

CHAPTER 8

This is what my Best Looks Like

I t was finally time to go to CU Boulder. I was very excited to attend my dream school, and visions of what college would look like were swimming through my head. According to the stories I had heard and the movies I had seen, I was certain that my time in college would be the best four years of my life. On top of that, I was doing what no one had thought I could do. I was going to Leeds School of Business at CU Boulder. I had a full-ride scholarship from the Daniels Fund in addition to a few other scholarships. I imagined making a group of lifelong friends, going to parties, and meeting girls, all while getting perfect grades. How hard could it be?

Well, as it turns out…pretty hard. Really hard. Harder than I had imagined, and harder than I could have prepared for. Here I was, intent on proving my greatness. Getting into CU Boulder as a Daniels Fund scholar was only half the battle. I knew I had to perform well, too. I struggled right off the bat with the demands of college classes. They are rigorous and nothing like high school. There are giant lecture halls and more complex content along with endless distractions right in the dorm hallways. It was too much.

The moment I started to struggle was the moment my ideal of college was shattered. I started to worry that maybe my high school counselor had been right. Maybe I wasn't cut out for college life. Maybe I wasn't going to succeed. I barely passed freshman year, which seemed to confirm my worst fears.

After a great summer traveling and then returning to Boulder for my sophomore year, I decided to change my attitude and fully embrace the college experience. It didn't help. My struggle heightened, and I realized I really wasn't enjoying anything. My peers, hall mates, and classmates all loved to party, and I started to despise the idea of a social life. But my grades kept slipping—so much so that I was put on academic probation during the first semester of my sophomore year. I'm talking Cs and Ds on my transcript. I still tried and gave it my all—only to turn up with the same results in second semester. If your grades don't improve while you're on academic probation, you get put on academic suspension. I suddenly realized that everything I had worked so hard for was at risk.

When I received my grades for second semester, I went to my advisors in tears. Luckily, I had already formed a relationship with my advisors, and they really respected and supported me. They understood my background, and they knew I wanted to succeed. I completely broke down in that office as the weight of reality came crashing down on me. This was it. My dream had been realized only shortly before it had been torn from my hands. It was bad enough that my idea of college was gone—now college, even as an experience, could be taken from me.

My advisors told me I did have one more chance: I could do summer school to make up what I had failed that semester. Then I could return in the fall on academic probation. If my performance still improved, I could get off academic probation for second semester of my junior year. I wanted to try it. I really did. But as I looked at my grades and remembered how hard I had worked, I once again broke down. "This is what my best looks like," I told them, my heart breaking. "This *is* my best."

But I continued to give it my best, and I did use the opportunity to attend summer school to try to get it right. From there, things started to change. My back was against the wall, and all I could do was my best, so I met with a tutor every day and doubled down on my studies more than ever. I realized that although college was not what I imagined it would be, I had to roll with the punches. There were so many opportunities to take advantage of outside the classroom as well. College, as an experience, is what preps us for success in the "real world." The way to make the most of it is to tailor it to what's best for us as individuals, which may take some trial and error. I made college the best it could be for me. Embracing that experience required learning and growth. It is by no means a perfect road. To learn, you have to encounter some trouble. To grow, you have to struggle. This is an inevitable fact of life. But if we embrace the obstacles, we have the control.

Ultimately, I realized that it wasn't a bad thing that college did not match my expectations. No, I didn't have straight As or the highest GPA—but that doesn't mean I didn't successfully complete college. Considering who I am, where I came from, and how hard I worked to not only get there but also get through, I'd say success is mine. I have to recognize my ability to get through a challenge like that as success.

Retrospectively, I realize how much it would have crushed me if I'd just given up when times got tough. I had worked so hard to get there, and I could easily have lost it all. I was so intent on proving to those who didn't believe in me that I could do what they didn't think I could do. I forgot about what really matters: the face looking back at me in the mirror. That defines what success means for me, because only I know what it took to get there. I think everyone should do the same. Just as our paths to greatness look different, our success looks different. It is unique. It is tailor made for us. That is greatness within itself: realizing who we are, what works for us, and giving our best—even if it may fall short.

CHAPTER 9

Congrats

Every time I share my life story, no one seems to think it's true. That confuses me. And I ask, "I just opened up to you. How do you *not* think this is true?" Often, their response is something to the effect of: "I can't believe that someone who has been through as much as you've been through could have turned it around and accomplished as much as you have."

I agree—my story is rare. But it is not impossible. And that's why I wanted to put it down on paper. The ups and downs of my life, as shared in these pages, should inspire you to go out into your life, too, and aspire to greatness.

After I share my story, listeners usually have a lot of questions. They're mostly curious about why I made the decisions I did along the way. I'm not sure I have an exact answer, except that I know I was put on this earth for a purpose. I know I felt a desire to fulfill that purpose. In order to do that, I had to follow my path to greatness. There were many distractions in my life that made that path to greatness hard to find. I could have traveled many different roads, but only one would lead me to greatness. The only way I could find that path was to follow my heart. Our hearts have the way. Our hearts act as our navigation system. My heart told me where I needed to go. It would have been much easier *not* to follow my heart, because so much was in front of me that I would rather have followed—an easier path, perhaps. Following your heart is typically the harder path to take, though, because it's more painful and re-quires going against the grain and being different. It means believing in yourself. It means doing what you think is right, even when others don't agree with you. It's hard to feel comfortable with being different and doing things in a different way.

But what was harder for me was not being able to see my destination. I had no idea where my heart was going to lead me. I was more comfortable with just following what I had seen in front of me, because at least then I was able to see the destination or what would happen. This invoked a deep-seated need for trust in my heart and trust in the path set out in my life. Not until I felt I had hit rock bottom and felt comfortable with giving it all up did I decide to give it my all and follow my heart's blind path.

And once I did that, everything started to change. Things began to fall into place over time. And there was something magical about it, because great things began to happen. I was able to remove the blindfold of distractions and limited belief. There was also the blindfold of labels—those placed on me, my life, my future—even my own labels for myself. And once the blindfold came off, I was able to see myself as successful. I was able to see myself living a fulfilled life and living a life of purpose.

Now, I know that this is just the beginning. I've come far, but I also have far to go. My life, with all its complicated pieces, was designed to be this way. It was uniquely engineered to allow me to thrive—obstacles, victories, successes, and all. My life is uniquely complicated for me and uniquely complicated in tune with my own greatness.

All I needed to do was realize my greatness and be in tune with it. Truthfully, other people did not understand. I would share my vision for my life and what I wanted, and everyone doubted me. They thought I was crazy. They thought I needed to be more realistic. I'm sure they talked behind my back. You'd think this negative energy would impact me in some way, but I kept in tune with my heart and my own uniquely complicated path to greatness, and I kept ascending.

And now, those very people who dissuaded and discouraged and chastised me have come to me and said, "Congrats." Those very people, who had I still been blindfolded could have swayed me off my path to greatness altogether, feel joy for my successes. They are willing to congratulate me—not only because they're surprised but because they have something to say congratulations for.

So instead of listening to how others can discourage you, remember that you have the ability to succeed on your own. Remember that one day, they will understand. You may have to show them first, but they will come to you in your victories and say, "Congrats."

CHAPTER 10
So What's Next?

My life is totally different today, but that doesn't mean I'm not still experiencing challenges. I could even say I'm experiencing more challenges now than ever before. They're just different challenges. Life isn't easy, but it's incredibly rewarding, and I have a great time with my life. It's important, though, to emphasize the difference between where I am now and where I was before. I am now achieving so much more than I originally believed I could accomplish or what others believed I could accomplish.

I feel that I have now arrived.

Many people didn't think I could even graduate, but I finished this book in preparation for my graduation from college. I'll be graduating with just three years under my belt and with two degrees in business. I was able to take something they didn't believe I could do and prove them wrong. I did it. I'm graduating in just three years, and as I'm graduating after such a short time span, I'm also saying that it wasn't easy. It was hard to accomplish this, and there were times in those big accomplishments that I didn't think I could make it through—and that's the point. My life today is so different than it was yesterday and the day before, but that doesn't mean I'm going to stop facing challenges. As I prepare for life after graduation, I'm pleased to announce that I'll be going to work for one of the largest financial institutions in the nation. Certainly no one believed that I'd be a business professional at this young age. So as I continue to talk about my accomplishments, sharing my story and teaching others is something that's near and dear to my heart. I feel I have a diverse perspective from my own experience and can impact the lives of people, not just in a personal sense but in a business sense.

I've started a successful business, and I plan to create more businesses—but what's most important to me is investing my time, energy, and financial resources into the community. I am now at a point where I am able to do so. By a lot of people's standards, I'm successful, but I have to say that by my own standards, I can't agree. I still have a lot of growing to do to continue on this path. I consider this to be only the beginning. Some may look at where I am now and see it as the end. They may believe that because I made it here, I can't make it any farther. But if I had allowed others' perceptions of me to sway the decisions I made and knock me off course, I wouldn't be here today. I certainly wouldn't be continuing on, either. If others' opinions mattered, I never would have cultivated the confidence or courage to step in the direction my heart was urging me. I never would have gone to college, and I never would have graduated.

Now that I have "arrived," I see this isn't as good as it gets. I see this as the beginning—and why would I let my beginning be my end? You can't let others' opinions influence you, no matter where you are on your path, because you'll get further when you pay no mind.

I will continuously find ways to impact the world in a positive way, and I won't stop until I feel in my heart that I have fulfilled my life's purpose. Sometimes I ask myself if I will ever get to that point. The honest answer is that I don't know…but what I do know for certain is that I will never reach that point by listening to another's opinion. What this comes down to is my parting message: you have to follow your heart.

I will specify that taking people's feedback and constructive criticism is different than being swayed by others' opinions. You need that feedback from those who see greatness within you, because they can really help. But if it's an opinion from someone who doesn't truly see the greatness within you, don't listen to it. When I talk about the people in my circle who have impacted me in a positive way, I see they are people who really believed in me and saw the greatness in me even when I didn't see it in myself. They did this via feedback that frankly I didn't always like. It was what I *needed* to hear more than what I *wanted* to hear—to get involved and do things outside my comfort zone. But they knew that's what I needed to do to get to the next step. Those are the opinions I respect, so I listened. I respect their ability to see greatness in me when I don't see it in myself. They see strength in me when I don't see it in myself. When they are continually pushing me, encouraging me, telling me that I have more to give than I had imagined, I see that they are making sure I get to where I need to be. They, too, see that this is my beginning.

CHAPTER 11
The Tipping Point

've come to a critical juncture. Even recounting all that
I have been through feels unfamiliar, somehow. I'm at
a pivotal point in my life, where many find themselves
after they have gone through as much as I have. But the
truth is, if I could do it all over again, I wouldn't change
a thing. I mean that. Because in recounting it, I realize
that even the moments that were small and seemingly

inconsequential actually played a big part in shaping who I am today. Everything happened for a reason.

I wrote this book because I think my life reflects a common story about someone who came from nothing and still made it. I hope you, the reader, can benefit from my story and find some meaning. I hope you can realize that if I can do it, *you* can do it, too.

The last twenty-one years of my life have been about building a foundation. I have come to know that the more we go through and the more we deal with, the stronger that foundation becomes. We prove what we are made of. And the stronger that foundation is to support us, the more we can build in our lives. Everything we've been through is the reason we can succeed as much as we can. We can decide what we want to build and start building at this pivotal point.

Tyler Perry's graduation speech talked about something similar. He said that in architecture and engineering, the foundation has to be just as wide and just as deep as whatever has been built on top. That makes sense, structurally. It puts everything into bird's-eye perspective. I realize now that I am truly on my path to greatness and that I can manifest my own destiny. I have accomplished more than anyone thought I could ever accomplish. I remember back when people thought I wouldn't make it to the age of eighteen, let alone graduate high school. I was told all the time to just get a job! Their view was that if I could at least start small and have some income, I'd have a chance at making it. But I wanted a degree…and I went on to get the degree earlier than expected. In fact, I got *two* degrees. That's what I built on top of my foundation. And when I think about what I want to build next, I realize it's about serving others.

I want my story to impact someone's life. I want you to know that when people tell you that you can't do something, it's almost always because they couldn't do it themselves. You can dream for *yourself*. But on the same note, when I tell you that you can do something because I've done it, you'd better believe that it means you can do it, too. *Because there's nothing special about me.* I'm not a genius or the "chosen one." Many of the people who make it this far aren't. I have no special talent. What I accredit my success to is my support system. It has grown over time, and those in the system have been there for me, giving me just enough support every step along the way to keep me from going over the edge. Don't be afraid to lean on other people while you're on your journey.

My life's work has been to find greatness in myself, to manifest my destiny, but also to be a resource to others by sharing my story. I can only share my story by my physical voice and presence to one group at a time. But with this book, I want you to know that I'm in your corner, too. You aren't going through this alone, and I hope you now consider me part of your support system.

Continue to surround yourself with people to pour into your foundation, because believe me, it's easy to give up without it! Even if you look around and feel entirely alone, remember that I am your support system. I want you to allow your heart to guide you and to remember that everything happening to you in your life right now is preparing you for what you're asking for.

I know this because I am still in the process of becoming the person I've always wanted to be—a happy person. A person who has fun. The path to getting here was nothing like I expected it to be. You don't always think that happiness can come from experiences of difficulties and challenges—but my perspective is different, because I realize now that all of that was preparing me for what I was asking for. And now, whatever the difficulties and challenges that greet me, I know the same—it's just preparing me for more of what I asked for.

So now I know I'm improving as I learn from my mistakes! Instead of loathing the difficult times and chastising myself for making mistakes, I can go easier on myself. I know that if ever a moment in life is too easy and I'm no longer experiencing any mistakes or challenges, that means I'm no longer growing. And we must continue to grow.

I don't have the same pressures now that I did in my earlier life, but by no means does that mean life gets easier. In fact, at times it may get harder, because we are building on a foundation. I can't ignore my past. But I'm committing to a life of challenging myself, stretching, and making mistakes—knowing that growth and fulfillment will come.

Removing the blindfold and seeing challenging times as necessary for growth and therefore fulfillment is a *growth mind-set*, one of two mind-sets I believe people can fall into. The other is a *victim mind-set*, in which people look at their situation and feel that they can't make it because of all that has happened to them. This is very much operating with limited beliefs, which sometimes leads to quitting.

But in a growth mind-set, one finds strength in the struggle and growth in the story. Imagine if you embraced all your challenges. Wouldn't that change the way you wake up and tackle life every day? It does for me. Keep the confidence and courage to follow your heart, even when it goes against the grain.

I see now that I've taken off the blindfold that it was equivalent to having a victim mind-set. When you can't see, you can't manifest destiny. I took small steps toward developing a growth mind-set—and you can, too. There were no large leaps. And I will continue with the small steps, being easy on myself. I must continue to follow the path my heart is guiding me to take.

You know, struggle has a unique way of making us who we are and who we will become. All high achievers share one quality: they are able to sustain effort, embracing the struggle and continuously seeing and realizing that it's preparing them for whatever's next.

So I'm no longer building the foundation—I'm building *on* the foundation. I have removed the blindfold, because I now have the courage to see.

You, too, will remove that blindfold and walk in your truth.

Realize your greatness.

EPILOGUE

My mom and me back in 1996. I was one year old, and she was thirteen.

Me and my grandma Brenda, circa 1996.

Me (age five) holding a church service and preaching to my cousins
in my bedroom at my grandma Brenda's house (2000).

Me (age five) dressed up on Sunday morning at church (2000).

Me (on the right), ten years old, with my best friend, Brandon, at the after-school program of the Boys & Girls Club (2005).

Me, age thirteen, dressed up and ready for the
eighth-grade formal (2008).

My dad (the man I aspire to be) and me, age eighteen,
at my Junior Achievement scholarship reception
during my senior year of high school (2013).

Me at twenty-one with my parents (who took me in during high
school) at the Boys & Girls Club 2016 Youth of
the Year celebration (March 2016).

Me at my graduation from CU Boulder with my
business degree in hand. I did it…I finished!
Class of 2016

A Letter from My Mother

To my son,

When I first found out I was pregnant, I thought it was a joke. How could someone so young, someone so little, a person still a child herself, be capable of having a baby? What would all of this mean? So many thoughts ran through my head. Not once did the thought of regret cross my mind. I was so shocked that all I kept thinking was "How?"

I knew that you weren't the mistake, but my actions came with consequences, whether good or bad. The day I found out I was pregnant with you, the doctor came in and told me there was some good news and some bad news. I asked her to start with the good news first, since I didn't really understand why I was at the doctor's office in the first place—other than a regular physical, your grandmother being the way she is. I came to learn that she had other reasons for why I needed to be there. The good news was that I wasn't that far along, and I could still terminate the pregnancy. The bad news was that I was already two months pregnant. I guess when you stop and look at it, it was all bad news at the time. The doctor asked for your grandma to leave the room. Once they left, she assured me that the decision was totally up to me, since it was my body. She patted me on my knee, told me she would give me a little bit of time to think about it, and then she left the room. After the door was closed, I dropped my head and began to cry and pray at the same time. There I was, all alone in this room, overcome by emotions and the decisions I needed to make.

When you were born, I had many mixed emotions. I was feeling hurt, disappointed, scared, happy, sad, and nervous. I felt every emotion you could imagine. The thought that continuously crossed my mind daily was "How am I going to be a mom at such a young age?" I decided to become a mother at twelve because of my religious beliefs, meaning that God wouldn't give me more than I could handle. If my Almighty Father in heaven looked down on me and trusted me with this big of a responsibility, then I had to know there was a reason for all this. I must say, I was very worried about how it was going to work out. I was only twelve—what did I know about being a parent? I worried about how people would look at me. I worried about what people thought about my mom. I worried about how this would affect the family. Most of all, I worried about finishing school. After all, I was only in the seventh grade...and preparing to become a mommy. I didn't care as much about what people would say. I expected that they would be talking about it. All things out of the norm are always talked about, and a girl only twelve years old having a baby was definitely not normal. They talked about Jesus. If it weren't for the support system that God had blessed me with, I don't know how any of it would have been possible.

Growing up, you were interested in a variety of things. The one I remember the most was your interest in musical instruments. You really enjoyed playing the drums. I thought you might become a musician. You always wanted to wear suits and ties and imitate the preachers in the church, so I even thought for a second that you might become a youth pastor, ministering to young males. You even enjoyed communion at church so much that you had your grandma go to the Bible bookstore to get you the representation symbols so you could partake at home. Being your mother has very much been a learning experience. You've truly taught me how to be a better mom for your younger siblings. You've taught me that no matter what your situation was or is, no matter where you've been or what you're going through, you can still overcome the obstacles. I don't feel like I was the always mother I could have been, but with the knowledge I had about being a parent, I feel I did the best I could. If only I would have known then what I know now. I had a disadvantage to start with. Thanks for not holding it against me!

Parents never stop worrying about their children, even when they're grown up. My biggest worry about you was that you would get caught up in the fast life—that you would get involved in gangs and that something bad would happen to you. If that happened, I could not have blamed anyone but myself. There would have been no one to point the finger at but me because of the environment I raised you in. I never stopped to think about how this would affect you. Son, I want to apologize for not putting you first. I made some bad choices in my life, but you live and learn. As a parent, you want your children to believe they can accomplish anything in life they dream of. I'm just sad to say that I never knew what your goals were. My prayers were always that you would be successful and do better in life that I did. C. J., that is one accomplishment you've certainly achieved. Son, you beat the odds! You're on the right path. Keep up the good work. I'm so blessed that God handpicked me specifically to be your mother. He makes no mistakes. I am so proud of the young man you've grown to be. What an honor to have someone so bright and intelligent for a son. I'm glad you belong to me.

I love you, C. J.

Love always,

Your mother

ACKNOWLEDGMENTS

To my mother: Thank you for the most incredible gift of all—the gift of life!

To Grandma Brenda: You have the biggest heart, and your love for me has been unconditional. You kept the bottom from falling out, and I thank you!

To Billy and Cathie Thompson: My parents! Mom and Pops! Thank you for taking me in and making me a part of your family and for truly loving me as your own from the beginning. You saved my life, and I am forever indebted to you.

To William Baird: Thank you for seeing the greatness in me when I didn't see it in myself. You stood up for me when others were in doubt. I'll never forget that. I wouldn't be here without you, brotha!

To the University of Colorado Boulder: Thank you for seeing me as more than a piece of paper. You gave me a chance when not many other colleges would have.

To the Daniels Fund: Thank you for giving me the opportunity to change my life. The reputation of your foundation and what it means to be a scholar has opened doors for me that would otherwise have been shut. I am forever grateful to be a part of the Daniels family.

To my dad: You are my dad. Without you I would not be here. I love you, man!

To Aunt Lisa and Aunt Nina: You don't get enough credit for what you do. You constantly pushed me out of my comfort zone. It's because of you that I found my passion for business and for giving. Thank you!

To Uncle Virgil: The memories of Kansas are extremely vivid in my mind. You always said you wanted us to be a contributing part of society, not a menace to society. I hope I've made your proud.

To Olivia Omega: I am blessed to have you on my team. Thank you for your continuous support and patience throughout this process. It has been a long time coming.

To Haley Hoffman Smith: Thank you for helping me discover the theme of my life and organizing the stories logically to complete this work.

To my mentors, advisors, and sponsors: You've always been there for me. Your way of support hasn't always been what I've wanted, but it has always been what I needed. I can't thank you enough for always believing in me.

To my family and friends who have impacted my life but whom I have not mentioned by name: I consider myself extremely fortunate to have you in my life and as a part of my story.

It takes a village. Thank you!

ABOUT THE AUTHOR

C. J. Manning avoided the gangs, drugs, violence, and mediocrity that claimed the lives of many of his childhood friends. He is an inspiring individual who now works as a speaker, consultant, and coach—passionate about helping others remove their blindfolds while empowering them to see their true potential and find their paths to greatness.

C. J. has overcome the odds and now shares the insights and life lessons his own humble beginnings have brought him, which he found to be key factors in his success. C. J. shares his unique perspective with his clients, passing along the wisdom he learned the hard way to help develop authentic leaders in business and in the community and drive them to achieve high performance.

C. J. currently resides in Denver, Colorado.

www.ingramcontent.com/pod-product-compliance
Lightning Source LLC
Chambersburg PA
CBHW031340040426
42443CB00006B/406